D0701485

SONGS FOR A SUMMONS

SONGS FOR A SUMMONS

poems

David Guterson

LOST HORSE PRESS
Sandpoint, Idaho

ACKNOWLEDGMENTS

The following poems were previously published, as is or in altered form, in periodicals, anthologies, and elsewhere:

Conjunctions: "Pavers," "Justification for Idleness," "Practice of the Ordinary," "Coyotes Calling"

Crab Creek Review: "Three Raccoons"

Narrative Magazine: "Birthday Card to a Son" (as "On His Twenty-Third"), "Pond of the False Prophet"

Pacific Northwest: "The Approach to the Pass," "Sunday Morning Monologue" (as "Time"

Ploughshares: "Teahouse"

Sawdust Mountain, Erik Johnson: "Closed Mill"

Seattle Post-Intelligencer: "The Fire Takes Its Second Life from Falling," "Four Notes to a Follower" (as "Trespass"), "Neighbors"

Seattle Review: "Escape"

Shenandoah: "Hiking Partner," "Fliers"

The Manner of the Country, edited by Stegner & Rowland: "Closed Mill," "Hikers," "Inheritance," "White Firs," "Neighbors"

Editor: Christopher Howell.

Cover Art by Ken Bushe. *Songs for a Summons,* 2013, 10" x 12", oil on canvas. This and other paintings by Ken Bushe may be viewed online at *www.kenbushe.co.uk.*

Author Photo by Tom Collicott.

Book & Cover Design: Christine Holbert.

FIRST EDITION

LOST HORSE PRESS books may be purchased online at *www.losthorsepress.org.*

LIBRARY OF CONGRESS CATALOGING-IN-PUBLICATION DATA

Guterson, David.
  [Poems. Selections]
  Songs for a Summons : poems / David Guterson.—First Edition.
    pages cm
  ISBN 978-0-9883166-9-0 (pbk.)
  I. Title.
  PS3557.U846A6 2014
  811'.54—dc23
                           2013045679

for Robin

CONTENTS

MONOLOGUES

INTERRUPTIONS

A TEST

This moment's previous to one more death.
Light rims the long clouds drifting in the west.
It's early spring and birds bare the stillness.

Which is more, death or birds?

SOLITUDES

POND OF THE FALSE PROPHET

The Pond of the False Prophet reproved me again
atop a headwall after the abandoned road
of the head razing hummingbird,
after snow retreat, minced bog, exposure, wild ginger.

Under Saint Peter's Gate, I thought I knew
water's wending and the last bench before the basin.
I thought I saw a different tarn, another lichen trace.
I put good foot after bad and, derided, I chased.

I carried as a porter carries dross.
I bowed, spent, beneath the talus face.
I lied to myself, I missed my way along the flank,
I was in the sun, I had a name, I called, I called on strength.

I constructed a day, a place, a voice, I kept my gait,
I made my gain. I poured the pebbles from my boots
and checked the reading I'd made, but the map
said otherwise, made obeisance to the ways,

and showed my grave.

ENTRANCE

In the morning my garret throws light on the ground
as if in parody of the house, a simulacrum.
I see it from the stairwell like a portal
to the world beneath the gravel.
Fled, flattened, cartesian—lid without a handle.
I dreamed these words, saw them only in passing.
The light behind the trees, like sand along a funnel,
comes once, converted into symbols
I've been saving out of fear of the ephemeral.
There's distaste to deleting, it's ineffective.
That door of light was off to the side
while I rose toward a last punctuating.
And meanwhile, my house stopped looming.
Newton's right about my clock—
I'll walk in Ireland next month
instead of leaping from the stairs.
Why underestimate awareness
just because it's out of style?
We go from where this ends with a final mark,
small but meaning what it means because.
I could have gone to look again
but I wouldn't have seen an entrance:
too late, not twice. I'd thrown myself in.

GROUP CAMPING

The spent match head's a black thorn preserved in wax.
In the well of flame, it's a clock face, eleven-thirty.
Another Saturday's guttered, almost—
guarded with a cupped hand,
and with something spacious in our part of the chart.
Drifted to our designations, we're compass points.
And as for me, the formal line bespeaks the cant,
indeed the worst, indeed asleep awake.
The one guest burgled at the inn
near Padua was the wandering American:
He'd desired privacy while the Romans faced the courtyard
and got drunk together. Should I blame myself
the candle's nearly fluttered shut?
A child's left behind a glowing necklace in the dirt,
harbinger or talisman? Four A.M.:
I take pains against the moment's loss.
Crows gather for what we've dropped.
They see me as I might be—
a lone watchman, a stay against darkness.
What do they know, feathers, bones?
Shouldn't we have tarried, feeding one fire?
Shouldn't we have gathered like addled sparks
whirling against the night?

THREE RACCOONS

One night, coming home, in hi-beams,
on their own, three kits,
at the start of fall,
watchful, if blind.

Two together, one behind.
Low in the interstices,
they do what they do,
which is to say, they live their lives.

The lagger hurries: am I death in a new guise?
They crouch to guess,
confront my rising eclipse
of their sight. I'm proof there's more

Than meets the eye—I'm light,
and on this treeless ribbon
dangerous entertainment—
I'm dazzling.

It's midnight—the silence of owls.
I sleep wearing my animal vestments.
These three now to the hilltop pond.
These three into the dark ravine, just beyond my sight.

DIAGNOSIS

He said it was good I'd come in early.
He said there was a week, or more, to decide.
A sunny afternoon, downhill to the city.
The light was dropping—one street mood.
On the busses people read or slept.
How pretty it all was that evening.

Later, I made tea and read the pamphlets on palliatives.
There was no point in pretending
to be Buddhist about it.
That night I saw my face in the mirror,
sick at the sink, pinched, cleaved.
Something plummeting in me.

I told her in the morning.
She was standing by our wheelbarrow
in the sun, disappointed.
Our roses were in need of pruning.
Our dog lay on the welcome mat.
A plane overhead suggested travel.

I fell not for immediate reasons.
It wasn't a diagnosis that sent me down.
I hurt, but no more than others—less.
Fate was here—
or call it what I willed.
Payment exacted in equipoise.

By late July, I was the same, but better.
We went to Naramata
and rode bicycles near the lake.
French-Canadians were picking cherries.
Experimentally, we sat on a terrace.
Below orchards, bluffs dropped away.

In August, my diagnosis seemed like life.
How good it was to stand in the heat
and smell the late rose rot in our garden.
From there I could see the row of birches
we'd planted just this side of the pond,
how they'd weathered a summer of caterpillars.

PLEA

I cleaned the glass before dawn.
I swept ash.
An hour of this on waking
reminded me of walking
the Elwha without you.
Next I tried laying my fire
without error, but the wind,
capricious in the flue, blew blasts.
Anything but meeting you.
I walked that way, apprehensive
about the days unaccounted for,
the minutes, too.
Downriver I cleared the trail of deer—
there was no time to sit under a tree
and talk to you. I misunderstood
and walked the seventeen miles
to Whiskey Bend instead.
So time passed and light came up:
variegated and volatile sky,
dying cedars, wind from the water.

I see what sort of day it was.
I conjured you in the odd moment,
lacking discipline but not desire,
conjured you on the far side of the river
calling above the din of water.
The banshee disguised,
the dark one, my destroyer.
Please, don't stay away.

MAIL

I got mail telling me
that mail was coming,
a package bigger than me
that would open me
before throwing me out,
a non-returnable return envelope
hinged like a maw,
a box into which I was born
to be fed. I got mail
saying what was coming
was not what I expected
but just what I'd ordered,
that it came without instructions
and delivered no deliverance,
that I would have to pick it up
at an unknown location
and sign for it in blood
before a magistrate
who didn't know my name.

And no, I couldn't return to sender,
pretend mine is the wrong address,
or tell the postman on his route to go away.

CLOSED MILL

Some of those trees are gone and some remain.
The mill, evaporating, has left behind moss.
There's a skein of cable amid blackberry
by the river—in the interstices of thorns,
seized chokers, a seized engine.
Even the sawdust mountain's blown
to where there's no evading nettles any longer.
I remember the morning the cook quit,
leaving his crumpled apron under warming lamps
while slabs of French toast smoked on the griddle.
I made enemies enough to color the future,
did what it took to stay on the wheel.
A friend wanted Jack Daniels in the hospital and got it.
Someone tried to hit me with a hammer.
There was nowhere to go and we went there together.
Returning's no worse than a bad dream, I think—
but I'm remorseful, now, about that running mill.
All those trees pushed loudly through the saw
in the era when I was king.

PAVERS

At first light
I'm laying pavers
with stinging fingers:
finding my grade.
The petals on the Frederick Minstrel fall—
spring snow in high country.

This work overcast with silence.
Hours pass.
Evening—I sit on pavers watching
the bubble in the level
as if air were absolute.
The straight line pleases.

Still, the fact is,
I'm wrong again
and what else is there?
I'll have to go back
to the skewed line and maul it in,
or pull the pavers out and lay them true.

INHERITANCE

When I lay his maps out on our bed
she asks me where I'm going.
There's too much topography
to keep my answer from getting lost in winter.
Fouled, old contours, creases eroded,
numbered but disorganized: maps of what?
I don't see maps.

Then my long-striding uncle
is laughing in his parka
while our tent howls off Mount Olympus.
Balloon-faced corpse laid out like Elpenor,
I have that, too.
Refusing to swim in Lake Billy Everett,
he napped instead.
He spoke what I was thinking when we played chess.
Dangerous, he said, to commit yourself that way.
The answer is, I'm going where he went.

NEIGHBORS

I'd like to move four stones and ten stumps
out of the field today, but right now silence is enough,
and fire, an answer for dread, a forgotten dream's distress,
guilt over solitude, the physics of stumps,
how to get a chain around one that won't slip off
or offer grief while not deluding myself,
stones, too, plus this regret at what I'm not doing
that might imply meaning, that odious filter,
and yet stones and stumps, their geometry and weight,
retain a superior claim, as does rising for a dying fire
to feed it fir from two storms back, when the road
was blocked by so many trees you couldn't pass
without a saw and neighbors sharing your condition.
Who else is awake on our end of the island,
wondering what to do before sunrise?

TEAHOUSE

In the dark field,
the question is the same.
Desiring to sit and not sit
in one place.

And write nothing about birds
with diaphanous wings,
how slow the elderly beneath spangled trees—
how thoughtful their retreat.

One bottomless pot.
But I can't keep Dōgen from my thoughts,
Tu Fu taking impressions of ferns,
the birds again,

hemlock tops, stockbrokers in a sunlit corner.
The shadow of my pen
meets the words, *Authentic peace is possible.*
On the far hill, rain over view houses.

THE FIRE TAKES ITS SECOND LIFE
FROM FALLING

God has invented so many scourges
I don't lift my tea cup without worship.
My morning fire's at full draw, but in the fog
coyotes say my house is empty.
My dog looks in the window as if to say
that fleas, sciatica, boredom, and dull food
are my responsibility, though I can't be sure
He doesn't mean to say I'm still asleep.
Geese from the south, their ephemeral discord,
heard but not seen, fading to the northeast.
The fire takes its second life from falling,
but when I rise to goad the flames
there's truth in my bones:
That birds know some chicks will feed kits.
Yet they're manic about nests,
and I wonder if they think their lives are short
and lack a fundamental rightness.
I'm thinking of baking a cake today,
and want to start separating yolk from white
while still feeling grateful for my pains.

WINTER SOLSTICE

One headlight's out,
a dream of deer obscures the road,
the sky's a canal,
between sleep and waking, out of fog,
a horseman rides,
disappearing at a glance,
and maybe it's the worn yearling
in the splayed and battered undergrowth,
the wet salal dashed,
the sluff of last year's bracken fern
now drowned, brown carnage,
and in the ditch where the emptied bag
of beer cans shines,
the ghosts of all my broken headlights
appear in sepia
at which I dare not look
on the hill toward home,
if it is home,
but could this be another life of mine
either not yet lived or not forgotten,
available in blurred shards only
on the darkest day of the year?

SAGES

The sages call you petal of a flower
in a rainstorm. They say you're sand
poured from a broad leaf when wind blows
upstream, or a stuck drake flapping in the yard
while in the gutter maple pods
cleave, or thoughts abrading time,
and sometimes the nails growing on saints
stuffed into cathedral walls.

But—I remember shaving in the driver's side mirror
by a pond in Normandy, and an eight dollar motel room
near Spokane in a heat wave.
We read sages there couchant,
and whatever those wise ones said about us,
we ate it with salt.
Plus, that pale mole to the left of your navel?
I'm not so naïve as to tell myself
the sages wouldn't have loved it painfully.

HIKING PARTNER

I went to find him lying in state
with a bursting face
and the mask of a pilot, flying at altitude,
not yet removed; propped like a dictator
on display. They said his heart had torn
in two and I should say what I needed—
now was the time—although, from what they knew,
he'd ceased. If so, what good to kneel
beside his long, blue frame, except for me?
I knelt and proclaimed, "Goddamn it," twice,
and his silent answer said more than nothing.
I heard then how he'd snored in Bear Pass,
stopping only to drink all his water
and piss beside our tent more loudly than he slept.
The next day, on the Elwha Snowfinger,
he'd sung ballads.

What's left is his parka with the broken zipper
and a hundred maps that, carefully examined,
illuminate the contours of his trail.

SHOOTING A RACCOON

Masked gambler rolling the dice for grapes,
I saw you in my sleep last night
at the moment of your death,
in the still fluid dream-light
with the last succulent skin of grapes
at your mouth. Sweet the little victory of surfeit
before your brain amid the leaves on the arbor,
white involutions,
was what was left this time instead of the fruit scat
you must have thought was so hilariously
an Up Yours calling card.
Well, it's easy to get pissed, but were you?
Maybe that was me, having already shot
incorrigible thieves out of the shed,
garbage-artists and investigators,
dog-slashers and all the climbers
I could discern, and having hung carcasses
from barn rafters out of faith in deterrence,
raccoons twisting on the summer air,
one with a coil of intestine between his legs.
Yet it's you I dream of, you staring up
my point-blank barrel shiny with burst grapes
I would have to say intelligently,
I would have to say with apprehension
in the half-second of my hesitation.
Grape-loving raccoon, I don't ask forgiveness
because there's no one to forgive,
but I do see your grin
in the moment before your brain stopped,
as if to say, "Aggrieved—that's you,"
with regret for my peril and ignorance.

A WALK

On a clear day, fog in the ravine.
I passed the unnamed outlet stream,
the six dying firs
and the gated lane to the forgotten orchard,
and I passed myself or what I
thought was myself
walking to town that morning
without a destination
and worse, without an end.
I'd have sacrificed breaths just then
for something to do that didn't seem wasted,
but by the bay, in shade,
there was no return.
Bees worked blackberries,
the woods had been razed.
The homes going up had already collapsed.
I saw my totems rotting on a hillside
after a fire had seared a forest
but well before the inevitable flood,
I walked through a cemetery
where an artist I knew had acquired a plot
as if a spot on earth meant something.
Nothing, not even the black hole
or dying star—I walked this way.
Old Mill Road should have been pleasant,
threading as it did among the living,
though even on the most innocent day
the dead press their case from every angle.
How pastoral, where goats had turned
a sea into a wallow. In every home and pasture,
eternal consolations, and much to do of import.
A mound of horse shit, for example,
though turning it escaped me.

Someone had forked it out of stables
probably after school,
but the horses went on dropping boluses
for her to spear, lift, and toss
while dreaming of recalcitrant boys.
I spilled onto the by-way,
thinking how easy it would be to wander
into traffic. A cur guarded wrecked cars near
mud flats and a mechanic in a greasesuit,
turning his tire iron, looked like a
Day of the Dead celebrant or a silhouette,
though at the same time I couldn't think
of anyone but me as I rounded the bay
where the Nichiren monks, beating drums,
gamely walked the other way.
I was in town now—the cineplex,
the car wash, the diner so authentic,
the museum for kids, the tavern
where boaters lined up on the Fourth.
To think all this mattered
no more or less than a mandala
scattered five thousand years hence
on the renamed remnants of the Ganges,
or the intelligent sufferer on a planet
close to this one writing odes to desire
while sipping *café au lait*.
Hey, stop telling me I can't imagine
how meaningless I am,
because I did that morning
on my way to the supermarket for—
but skip it, please.
I wasn't thinking any more.
I'd walked my long miles and arrived.

PRACTICE OF THE ORDINARY

Another day so quiet it's easy to think of dying
as an organizer, as an advertisement
for financial expertise on a remote lake
reserved for people with enviable marriages,
as matinee cinema, as walking
where it doesn't need to be raining
or not raining, a sidewalk is sufficient,
the parking lot at Target, pie's an obvious inciter,
I'm certainly not the only patron at Applebee's
enjoying pie while thinking about dying,
maybe for the twelfth or fifteenth time in an hour,
those narrow fifty-mile-an-hour lanes
between the mall and the Interstate
full of crazed teenagers also thinking about dying,
but not in the same way I'm thinking about it
because they're so eroticized,
though it should be noted here
that they're suicidal, too,
still capable of the romantic view, and fierce.

Outside my window, fruit trees are blooming.
I should thin their buds but, putting things in order,
there are two fallen trees in the field
that might get mixed up with the long grass
if I don't go now in the name of the brush hog.
Still, what I would really like to do today
is clean the shop, which I think with patience
might be done from a wheelchair.
The sole purpose of a moment's death.
What's easy now will be hard later.
Everything I do could be practice.

THE GREAT CHAM

It turns out that was my youthful bent:
Pepys one day, Johnson the next.
But the Great Cham knew better
than to walk in the Blue Mountains.
Tiring of that lofty Augustan
I went forth brimming; myself instead.
I put our baby on my head
for our walk to the escarpment.
The bush gave way to banksia.
We stood on the cusp
and talked westward, amid vines.
The world was shorn of distance but not gloss.
No one knows what Johnson said in death,
though Boswell reports it was
"God bless you, my dear,"
to a girl who'd come to his chamber
on a mission. "God bless you, my dear,"
the Great Cham might have said,
finding his subject at the end.

MONOLOGUES

MARS: A SUMMATION

"We can say of Mars—what can we say of Mars?
That Confederated Mars disastrously lost its scruples?
There's evidence for this, though of course it's truncated.
A prevalent counter: The Martian atmosphere deteriorated.
Yet still the Great Shunning is worthy of a paper.
Why study Mars? There are various heated answers.
Well, we're out of time, that's irony for you.
An Elegy for the Red Planet is tomorrow's lecture.
Reading is *The Red Planet: A Retrospective*
and—don't forget, please—*The Martian Poetry Review*."

CONDEMNATION FROM A BUDDHIST

"Emptiness, turned from, remains form.
Hiding in the desert requires sand.
Exulting backfires, sorrow's injurious,
safety's dangerous, and theater's dire,
because the part you play, for yourself,
out of fear, is the ostrich of apocrypha,
the bird of flightless folly.
So be it—this life you perform.
Your doctor treats your desolate face,
your porter hauls your kit to the inn,
but still no remedy for your suffering,
which isn't fooled by your shouting.
A Right Thought—
I wouldn't want to be you, either,
by which I mean we agree.
And don't think compassion's a cryptic smile,
because a Buddhist isn't the sap
you want him to be.
Just keep moving from illusion to illusion,
adding cement to your house of cards,
since being you isn't fruitless,
it's how you're redeemed."

REPORT

"My Liege:
The dream of triumph is a soluble set of ramparts.
On the water, barbarians of a tenor you haven't seen.
And you with your striving and estimable behavior
while to your citadel she lays siege.
Oh General and King, you've read enough
to know the fatal flaw's not desire but defense,
yet shield high you'd meet her on the plain below
for one last feint. My Lord Supreme, I speak
for your sake on this field of final prey:
You stinking, earthly warrior in dust,
you know how it must be. She'll parry with,
In deadly earnest, then, let's clash,
and send forth a harrowing heroine with a mirror,
dedicated to your defeat."

HOLISTIC PRACTITIONER: PSORIASIS

"I sense in your liver too much defensiveness—
as if your skin was a wall made thicker by threat.
Or a curse: when your fear and doubt wax,
they do it at your elbows and knees,
and at those telling spots that add to your disease—
the corner of your eye, snow in your ears,
both of which you feed.
Short sleeves are out, if you want to be petty,
so it's a reminder, this flame—do you?
Although for long periods you forget you have it.
Benign enough not to shorten your years,
it keeps returning with a message—
that you're making too much heat
or living on a tangent, working at the wrong job
or running when you might just dream.
In short, met earlier we might have mastered your disease,
but after too many years it's wrong to hope for that
and therefore you must accept your fate.
Hear—please—what psoriasis means:
That like the rest of us you have to live inside your skin."

FOUR NOTES TO A FOLLOWER

"Yes, I can tell you
of the cold on this journey,
how it begins—
with much quartering to wind.

And it's not snuffed matches
along this frozen tract,
it's that you lost them first.
No sign, no prints.

I didn't set out like this.
I made shelter,
slept in the lee of ice,
rose, took readings in mist.

A winter journey, tracks swept away.
You may never get back
if you don't turn now,
into your own south wind."

NO HUNTING: AN EXPLANATION

"Twice I bought boxed birds mail order
and shot them for the edification of dogs.
I hammered quail in asparagus.
I banged so many ducks off a smoking slough
a hawk had time to eat the breast of one
before I picked it up.

Chukars roused against a blinding light,
migratory doves, flaring teal,
friendless Huns,
widgeons under low-lying fog,
sharptail wanting speed.

And I remember the frozen decoys,
and the pea in my whistle, stuck.
The dog's withers barbed-wired and
the bloody pastern.
The broken glass on the reservation
and the moods of waterfowlers
awake at noon in folding chairs, waiting.

Training in the loneliest of canyons,
I dizzied hens up one by one
and stuffed them under sage,
worried, for the dog's sake,
about water, sun, and snakes.

One afternoon, a plunging pheasant hit my
shoulder after spiraling and vaulting.
The time I potted a grouse point-blank
there was little left save stench.
Stung by bees in a thicket, I struck my head on a log,
but nothing changed and I didn't wake up.

I've wasted time. The flush of birds remains
the same. Up they come—in coarser light—
I just was never ready for their flight."

THE PROCRASTINATOR'S LOGIC

"Twenty years of health problems
ending in a painful death is not uncommon.
The live trap presses the mouse between walls.
Lemon-herb chicken under heat lamps, $7.95,
what a battle you fought!
They pulled his fingernails out when he wouldn't talk,
then buried her in salt. Disemboweled, we had to watch.
Most do it in a lonely corner, turned away from noise.
A night in a charnel house could straighten us out
or call a halt, but just as often, life seems fine,
we're not distraught and think instead of getting laid or lunch.
Why not? There's plenty of time to die just once,
so later is the time to give it thought."

THE ANCIENT MARINER'S RETORT

"You've cut me deep.
The rend when what I wanted was to sleep.
I don't ask for much, just peace,
if peace you could construe it as—
will you? As opposed to asking for a new milieu
of fires I would put out one by one?
To do, now, what you say I've left undone
is to upset my apple cart,
when really it's an axle, for my part,
that needs a lift and nothing more.
To put things right or walk right through the door
you're opening: I'm an old dog, no new tricks,
could you leave me be, please, retrieving sticks
as I have always done with much success?
In my case I'll make do with less and less
and then expire. Evening's not the time
to catch a ship, after all, except the one departing
from life's slip. Let me go as I have been, then.
If you have to bring it up again, that's contrary
to my sense of meaning well for me.
Meaning well's a dipped oar, boy,
for sailors putting out to sea,
as I am putting out still free
with sounding weight and cross-staff.
Write that on my epitaph.
Leave me my tools, I'll navigate, you pull.
The tide even now is nearing full
and already we are running.
Granted, I've never had the cunning
it takes to plumb, but I've had the grace
to travel straight which is a plus.
Boy, I go my way both early and late.
Is not my rime about a voyage and a wreck?
I wear the albatross about my neck—
by God—by choice."

POLONIUS TO LAERTES: AN UPDATE

"One, don't try to solve every problem
before you go, as it's good to have some problems
on the road—a couple of infected toes,
for example, would compel you to search
for an antidote.

Two, 'travel light,' so burdensome.
No maxims, then, or mantras—no axioms.
Be weighed down, confused, grope.

Three, no hardships made.
You only embarrass yourself and us that way.
Dangle above a real abyss, don't play.
The world's not your game.

Four—but should there be a Four?

Five, imagine that on the road to Pokhara
a beggar tells you the bottomless bowl fable—
will you empty your wallet or invoke this Five?
That form, emptiness, emptiness, form—
to know this is to wake, to be alive."

BIRTHDAY CARD TO A SON

"You are on a dream journey
with no one on your right.

You are on a journey
out and back again.

Take the path on the left
because it is the wrong one.

The stone you carry
doesn't matter.

In the end, death will be unnerving.
Greet it with consideration.

It is worthwhile to contemplate
the emptiness of form.

When the last leaf is off the tree,
celebrate illusion.

All my words are false, of course,
since there are those I painfully adore."

LETTER FROM MY OLD FRIEND THE POET

"Where the Goldberg *Variations* meet Planck's constant
the mind of God has a heart attack.
Sprawled, we tried to say *schist* as He would
between the rivulets in the Valley of the Silent Men.
The dreams of Babylon were fours on scales of one to ten
and fives on Vesuvian scales. No, I never made it to the Ludden-Scott
Saddle, never got up a river without regret.
They asked for the Argentine's opinion of Schopenhauer and, lying,
she said she'd never been there. Barkeep got peeved when we ladled
Zulu beer, she was a geisha-in-training, remember?
That time we rode the Greyhound to Krakatoa with complimentary
bagged lunches? While listening to Gould or Tears for Fears?
That time on the taiga, popping grubs like shelled peanuts?
And you thought the auto parts store was a steakhouse.
You'll probably be gingered these lines don't rhyme—
fixed in your sensible nick of time."

PSYCHIATRIST'S EXAMPLE

"We pay dearly for a glimpse in loss:
After much consideration and talk,
Narcissus drew back and said, 'That's me,'
rose and walked into a mirrorless sea,
wandered in a hall of mirrors,
faced himself egregiously,
shed tears and watched himself thin at the lip,
asked for a reprieve, dislocated his hip,
threw out his back and, after that,
got told chemotherapy was his return ticket.
That's if in lieu of an early exit,
infamy as an aspersion, beauty's apparition,
if in lieu of rotting in the weeping lake
or lending his name to a jonquil or a rake,
Narcissus understood his reflection."

SUNDAY MORNING MONOLOGUE

"All morning I've threatened
to do something nameless
and, desiring to desire,
ignored good advice:
to read the sutras
like everything depended on it.
I've let languor in
like there's time to name names
or seconds to dismiss looking forward.
Watching the toaster's an option,
but so is putting it back in the cupboard.
If I'm choosing between myself
and the world, is that a vain consideration?
The prospect of travel next week
shouldn't overwhelm my morning,
since I might be dead before New Jersey:
no itinerary for that.
Last night I dreamed of an earthquake
which, with an effort, I took seriously.
There are mouths to feed, I'm sure of this.
I watch my daughter drink tea
while wrapped in a blanket and think
keeping to the middle on clear mornings isn't easy.
What else should I do while being human?"

THE DIASPORA OF THE POETS: A LECTURE

"The diaspora of the poets pre-dates Plato—
their journey from the desert of beauty
to the abyss of truth was foretold
by the prophets of antiquity.
A further supposition holds
that aliens planted poets in the Antediluvian,
that they were meant to be gleaned
in the perilous future, seed poets rising
rank on rank to lead us
from this dream we're believing.

Or maybe the poets are ensorcelling prophets—
flying free like demons,
they coalesce our fate by setting music to it.
Some poets obey the sea and sky,
God's voice be His mood foul or fair,
or succubi (remember the Romantics).
Or they dip into the shaman's Lethe
to feed us loaves and fish filets,
or, like chefs and alchemists,
they're good at making something out of nothing.

The surface of a pond when muddied poets clarify
while off their game, some poets stir septic tanks
with divining rods, some dive in to swim
among the frogs and touch the spongy eggs of frogs—
I've seen a poet climb a tree and top it,
another scuttling heavy equipment,
a third versifying the others in their cups.
But as I say, these poets have been traveling
in their holy caravel since time immemorial,
and stop, in our year, only for the nonce."

INTERRUPTIONS

APRIL

The walls cant and the latches sink.
Our garden, which seems so tranquil,
is full of strain.

Nesting ducks don't want to fly
from swimming dogs, but what choice
do they have this morning?

It's too late—the blackberry's gone green.
I pulled what I pulled
in the time I made.

Down the field, low sod sits wet,
a boon for mosquitoes
and the swallows of the evening.

Last night I left my shovel by the pond.
I left dreams in the shed,
and darkness is my wake.

Spring: I wake up fast.
I need to groom where I pulled stumps—
it's time to plant.

COYOTES CALLING

At dusk the frogs are loud enough,
less rhythmic than crickets,
calling the raccoons.

I didn't look for the moon tonight,
but my daughter's right about the willow
in the dark. It shouldn't be seen by me alone.

In the greenhouse today a swollen bee
worked the glass. I watched it
while looking for a handful of string.

It's spring. A mallard hen and drake,
in rain, flew down the center of the road
toward the stream.

Soon the garden voles will take the field.
Each year, the same—
fled, they return.

Today I lifted my shovel carelessly.
My mind went to the spider
in the corner of the cart.

I shoveled in a dream instead of shoveling,
but now and then a worm woke me
with the opportunity not to end its life.

And maybe, dying, I'll hear coyotes calling.
Will it be enough then to say that I lived this way,
pursuing my salvation haphazardly?

EXITING THE BARDOS

It's a moment of regret,
finding parents.
You wake up in the old realm.

Was your will honored?
Imagine all the lovers on the night in question
seeing God on His distant shore.

You fall in. Lathered, rank with one another,
those two chuff like fish on a deck
and return to their sheets and opened door.

Thus are you bound again
with your burden but no staff.
Love, you sojourner, is your way back.

DHARMA BUM

Boat on the water—
a treble note, fading.

In the new light, it's clear:
we're moving toward rain.

Fallen flowers on the table—
night has laid them under.

Already I'm foolish enough
to have hopes for the coming hours.

My morning tea's rich,
superior to other things.

I cling to the dancers
and the cruel remark.

I haven't overcome the applause
or the hearse.

My waste bin's full of pleas.
I think about my needs.

Deposited on the shore of waking, alive,
a mayfly, like me, has all day.

TENSION OF EQUIPOISE

Dispassionate equality of sunrise and sunset,
rose thorn and stigma,
and from an unlit house, the visible dawn.

Between I depend on habits,
on the timely appearance of shadows
and ghosts, and on poems.

No past or future,
but still I want to feed my dog
to have done what must be done.

Yesterday, I was drawn to land.
Buffeted by sleep, that steep intervention,
today I'm drawn to water.

Up from the well now,
in this second half of life.
Today I'm pushed forward and drawn back.

THE APPROACH TO THE PASS

The trail goes where the guide said it would.
I cross a blowdown and find it on the other side.

Lost again, I see through trees
a world of clouds.

Why this loneliness? What good does it do me?
For company, two camp robbers.

Climbing ice to the frozen lake,
I wonder what fleas are these that thrive in so much snow.

Drawn out of the wind,
I darn a sock with cold hands.

Last night, goats made a visit on the full moon,
demanding salt in toll for my dreams.

Now it's morning—the earth didn't stop.
I have to go on, and cross that pass.

JUSTIFICATION FOR IDLENESS

Because tomorrow illuminates itself,
this autumn day is disposable.

One thing and then another,
and then one day, not another.

Like a thousand leaves in a storm,
my thoughts rake all the leaves they can find while others fall.

Leaves, please demonstrate how to waste time carefully.
Let me go as you do, down, naked to the wind and rain.

BARTHES AND BARTH

For years I looked at the page.
I took a knitting needle to a drying sock.
Light interpenetrated trees.

One post only at a time went up.
My pen stood propped.
Demons manufactured dreams.

Between a puddle and my glasses,
loss accrued. "Defenestration,"
assorted banes.

Dying soldier calling "mum,"
caged gorillas nulling mates:
untimely visitors, stragglers, estranged.

And in the annals of personal futility
I ran in slow motion,
put boxes away.

Roland Barthes and John Barth,
doorkeepers of meaning:
I add their names.

EXPANSES

FLIGHT

All night we shuddered through the earth's
exhalations not quite as strangers,
certain to miss connection
and wondering what the lights
at the ends of the wings said
in their loneliness, in the torpor of altitude,
while one attendant rubbed her arches
in the galley and another mulled
his terrestrial paralysis,
his fiscal trauma and emptiness,
up and down the rows
we flew discomfited by projection,
so much fidgeting along the dark aisle
it's as if we were ants or bees *in extremis,*
hurling ourselves against glass
to the drone of a retarding clock
while first-class read Bolaño at his height.
The pilot thinks of the straining button
at the breast of his porn site Goddess of Wisdom,
the unaccompanied minor watches
Snakes on a Plane mentally,
the poet with the saxophone hallucinates
Trungpa while migrating from Greece—
how is this any different from living?
Sad artists with disappearing canvas,
seatbacks in the meditative position,
we're reconciled to air under and over
our wings, and bound to flight.

WHAT HAPPENS IN VEGAS

Goes away.

Viva Las Vegas! It's the Bombay Boys and the Bewilderment Posse
in a show-down at the Center for the Sacrament,
plus seven-to-one the gunslinger from Evanston
is really there in twenty minutes. At her homework in the hold,
she's a paratrooper waiting for the call to jump,
but needs time to close her books, too, and strap in
with a secondary. Why not a simulated Red Light District,
with disdainful Amsterdamer whores reading Robbe-Grillet
in canisters, wouldn't that give us more than we got?
But post-post-something-or-other the irony's turned "tragic,"
and now we have to pray for the Gangster of Love
to come out from among the hypnotists and magicians,
and for Carrot Top, diced, at the Buffet of Qualms,
and for the woman who said I should go fuck myself
when I asked her if she would shut up during O.
Here, this goes out to the girl throwing up on the People Mover:
You're loved, your job is waiting for you, and you'll be back next
year stronger for the experience,
not unlike that of The Awakened One
hanging from his rope bed in the sal trees when he realized
that the way to die was on his right side with his hand
supporting his head. There's golden nuggets all up and down Vegas,
and plenty of thoughtful and contemplative souls
driven by melancholy into friendliness toward strangers;
you mostly see them on their way to work, obstinately sad
beneath a clean sun, smiling, too, and pressed to let you know,
in code—as if you and they were complicit, fellow Gnostics—
that they want you to have a nice day in Vegas,
that they believe you can figure out how to arrange this
but that's it's their job to indicate the possibility exists
and to get you started on the road toward their hometown's
encrypted, simpler satisfactions.

That's sort of like Jesus the Hermaphrodite, appearing live
at The Palace of Nirvana for one week only
between his several Eastern European engagements,
though there's always the chance he'll return to Caesar's Palace
after the flash-flood but before the snow flies. Viva Las Vegas!
We got ferried in, ferried out, and, in between—shook.
De-pocketed and bank-shot to a frazzled T. They made fools of us
in Vegas, fiddled and diddled us according to their paradigm.
We were like Rosencrantz and Guildenstern at Luxor,
the Bellagio. Somebody suggested that if I had to visit,
it was best to ignore Vegas, eat good meals, take the sun,
take offense, pretend I wasn't in Vegas while in Vegas,
but then—why go? I went, got fleeced, made hay,
and panned for gold, I sold and got sold, they put me
in the hole—I lost and won like everybody else.

WORN FLOOR

I wore the floor out under my desk,
sanded lying on my side,
just no more shards of floor in the feet, please,
that's all I sanded toward.

Off Soho Square, in Hazlitt's house,
the floors are at this hour unreadable.
Scratched, dinged, sanded, oiled,
planed, honed, buffed, ignored,

They're fodder for conjecture, boards to brood over.
But look: your fellow guests are eating scones
where Hazlitt died, at 52,
still hoping for one more essay.

BAKERY

I say to a baker, "Things could be worse,
what with the tins and the smell of warm yeast,
and the solitude at dawn while it rains outside."
But should I speak of his art in these cadences?
It's out of bounds, maybe, something better left
unsaid so as to leave it pure.
Maybe I should mention weather,
draw us back while he's drawing hot water:
Darkness and rain as darkness and rain,
thick traffic on Fourth Avenue South.
Clam up because I've said things irredeemable,
fall back on being twice his age
and cryptically prone to different rules.

But then while I'm eating an exemplary scone,
fetishizing black tea, eyeing troubling news,
no one in this bakery but two willful loners,
he comes in his apron to stand by my table,
and suddenly like a moonlighting philosophy student—
a sensitive soul, soft-spoken, well-read—
asks me if everything's all right.

FLIERS

Three times this eagle stoops to pluck entrails.
Myth's no better. In gray branch lattice, alone—
as vultures haunt centurions.
The blue heron's invisibly just so,
the swallows fresh to flight,
thrush sate in mow rise, tree set in motion by a watchful eye.
Hawk-hunted hedge-runners, riders of the wave and particle
at midnight. Death all day long, with song:
A goose hit the house and we larded her with optimism.
Apple-stuffed, rank, collected from a bulb bed.
It's Christmas in July. Riven, thrive. Drilling flicker,
seed on, dent the gutter. The hawk's materializing flare,
the bowerbird's bombast, the lek below snowline
on a hillside, the dire molt. Just after clouds pass,
the falcon strikes. And maybe it's so:
The dead don't want us back or miss our clutch.
But in their dreams they're flying, too and,
doomed for return, plunge—hard—into this life.

CANINE EPISTEMOLOGY

"A dog barks" speaks of it,
but if I say "A dog barks" to a dog
it's only heard if he's not deaf.

My dog's partly deaf,
so I have to yell to be heard;
still, even if he hears me, am I me?

And as for yelling: if I yell
it might be to him like barking is to me,
or at least I think it might.

We might say that at the very least
my conditionals *are*,
even if I'm *not*,

That much we might get comfortable with—
or not—but once again, each dog
puts things in a different shade of light.

THE INFANT

Of all the animals blind at birth,
people see farthest.
To be born human's a window
and blindness a practice.
In the old stories, it's the sightless who see.
So if on waking you're adamant
about the light behind your eyes,
that could be wisdom, strength, or a test.
Maybe your way to know all's well is eyes shut,
trusting love like a bird in its nest,
mouth open, asking to be fed.

MATE

He had in him the want of touch—the need to be met.
Tearing up his face each morning and holding the list.
To have her smell and the smell of kids,
extract a kiss, exacted a price, demanded *sturm* and stint.
Yet he did much musing on the trials of men—
the finer, brooding compensations.
Worked for himself with prudence but impatience.
No bill unpaid before the nap, his closet spare,
nothing untoward except his mean game of chess.

Now, of course, his prior moves insist.
It was not and never was what his opponent did.
His running King got tipped by volition.
It's there in the notation, in code, in print,
that mid-match he made his final commit.
A last chance, before his end-game.

ESCAPE

She awakens house-bound. It's disorienting.
This isn't the warmth that augurs gathering.
Knowing something's off's a burden.
Better to finish winter as encoded;
now she's a glitch, like if you and me forego our soma.
Bristling, she's inconsolable at the window—
just let me past the Archons—
while weeping at the one apparent aperture.
Whatever prayers mean, then,
could she have predicted my higher power
lubing up of glides with heavy-duty silicon?
Did she know that fleeing meant finding winter—
that season without solace?
Out she goes, rising, to her new life of dying,
one fleeting free triumphant spark.

WHITE FIRS

They didn't like wet feet is their epitaph—
snag klatch of white firs across from the gate,
down from the bull rock dumped by the stream,
near where a neighbor re-starts his siphon
with a generator and pump in a van.
Gradually they came to ask against the sky,
ivy refused them, sticks clashed and dried,
and sometimes I thought they looked like men—
stolid, accusatory, questioning.
They set themselves off with their leafless June fretwork,
fell in winter, cold with disregard.
Those still remaining stood among the heaped
like final pieces on a chessboard.
We called them piss firs for their stink when mauled,
but they were no good for burning
and held whole ponds—so why did they drop
unannounced? Not even owls dignified their silhouettes.
They were freight cars on the ground, wrecked.

The last wretch fell in the road Monday morning,
and the UPS man, stopped, explained,
"This thing's in the way. Too heavy to move.
I've put in a call. They're bringing a saw.
They'll clean it up and we'll get through.
All of us have things we have to do."

OUT OF JOINT

As if traction could ameliorate our condition
by aligning jarred intersections in a frame,
like a patient with one leg dangling from two pulleys,
we're helpless, joined to nothing
and to talk of nothing.
How welcome the sedative,
welcome the memory of a prior decade,
prior millennium of another feeling:
Trip to Ellis Island or Statue of Liberty,
chicken feet in Chinatown,
salted chestnuts on the esplanade.
Whereas now strained, tender, inflamed,
hobbled by our dislocation,
we're angry at our embittered selves,
since we know we have to be here,
paying for innocence with an injury
we didn't imagine
but which is now incorporate and mundane.